THE NORMANS AND THE ANGEVINS
1066–1216

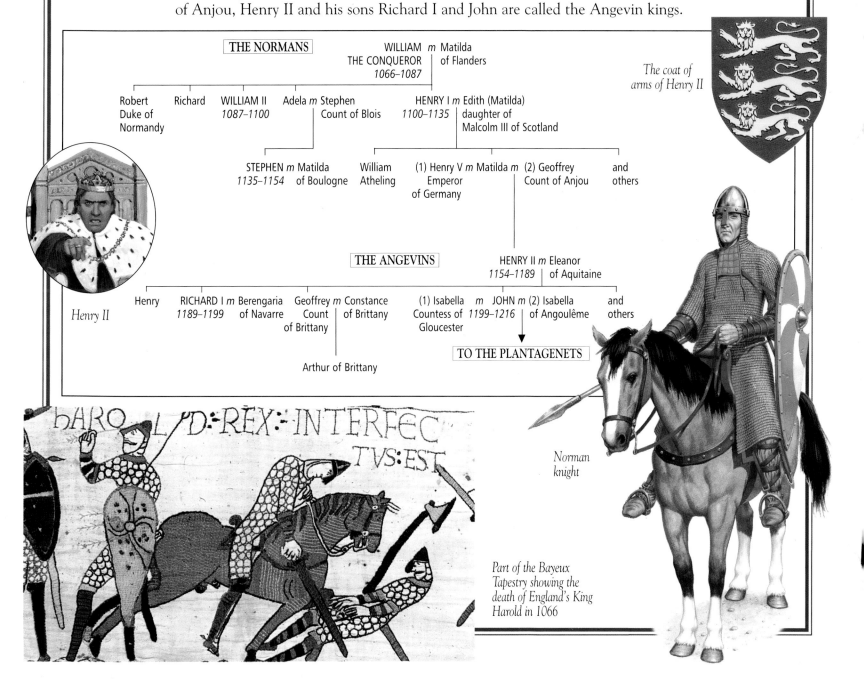

William the Conqueror

The coat of arms of William the Conqueror

William the Conqueror and his Norman troops were the last foreign soldiers to invade England. It took many years for the English people and their French-speaking lords to become one nation. William had to build strong castles to keep order — one still remaining is the Tower of London. Two of his sons became king: William II and then Henry I. After Henry's death, the supporters of his daughter Matilda fought those of her cousin King Stephen for years, causing great suffering in England. Peace was restored by Matilda's powerful son Henry II. Because Matilda had married the French Count of Anjou, Henry II and his sons Richard I and John are called the Angevin kings.

The coat of arms of Henry II

THE NORMANS

WILLIAM THE CONQUEROR *m* Matilda of Flanders
1066–1087

Robert Duke of Normandy — Richard — WILLIAM II *1087–1100* — Adela *m* Stephen Count of Blois — HENRY I *m* Edith (Matilda) daughter of Malcolm III of Scotland *1100–1135*

STEPHEN *m* Matilda of Boulogne *1135–1154* — William Atheling — (1) Henry V *m* Matilda *m* (2) Geoffrey Count of Anjou — and others
Emperor of Germany

THE ANGEVINS

HENRY II *m* Eleanor of Aquitaine *1154–1189*

Henry — RICHARD I *m* Berengaria of Navarre *1189–1199* — Geoffrey *m* Constance Count of Brittany of Brittany — (1) Isabella Countess of Gloucester *m* JOHN *m* (2) Isabella of Angoulême *1199–1216* — and others

Arthur of Brittany

TO THE PLANTAGENETS

Henry II

Norman knight

Part of the Bayeux Tapestry showing the death of England's King Harold in 1066

hARO L D REX INTERFEC TVS EST

GEORGE V
1910–1936
George had to lead Britain and her colonies through the terrible First World War. In his reign women obtained the vote.

GEORGE VI 1936–1952
Edward's shy brother never expected to become king. He mastered his stammer and during the Second World War earned the country's warm affection.

ELIZABETH II 1952–
The wise, dignified and hard-working Queen Elizabeth II is the figure-head of the nation. Long may she reign!

EDWARD VII
1901–1910
Edward was a jovial man, fond of horse racing and of good food (his mother had disapproved). He was popular with the people and helped to keep Europe at peace during his lifetime.

EDWARD VIII
1936
Edward was a modern-style prince, but he was never crowned. He chose to give up the throne rather than the woman he loved, Wallis Simpson, whom some people would not accept as his queen.

	GEORGE V 1910–1936		GEORGE VI 1936–1952	ELIZABETH II 1952–
EDWARD VII 1901–1910			EDWARD VIII 1936	

SAXE-COBURG GOTHA 1901–1910

THE HOUSE OF WINDSOR 1910–

GEORGE III
1760–1820
Father of 15 children, George III was a much-loved king for 50 years. During his reign Gainsborough and Reynolds painted, Sheridan wrote plays, slavery was abolished in England and Australia was colonised.

GEORGE IV
1820–1830
George ruled as Prince Regent during his father's long illness, when Britain was fighting Napoleon. He built the fantasy palace, Brighton Pavilion.

WILLIAM IV 1830–1837
William joined the Navy as a 13-year-old and enjoyed life at sea. Later he became known as "the Sailor King".

VICTORIA
1837–1901
By the end of her long reign Victoria was queen of a confident, powerful, industrial Britain, which had grown rich from its many overseas colonies.

GEORGE II
1727–1760
George II, like his father George I, preferred Germany to England but, unlike his father, he learned to speak English well. He loved music and encouraged the great composer Handel.

GEORGE III 1760–1820	GEORGE IV 1820–1830	VICTORIA 1837–1901
	WILLIAM IV 1830–1837	

1714–1901

THE PLANTAGENETS AND THE HOUSE OF LANCASTER
1216–1471

Henry III

The coat of arms of Henry III

Most of the Plantagenet kings had to struggle against their nobles who wanted more power. Henry III's reign saw the first-ever Parliament in 1265 — the forerunner of today's House of Lords. (There was no House of Commons until much later.) Henry's son Edward I, a fine soldier, brought Wales under the English crown. He tried to conquer Scotland, too, but failed, as did his son Edward II. In Edward III's reign, a plague called the Black Death (1348–1350) killed one-third of the British people. Richard II, grandson of Edward III, was forced off his throne by his cousin Henry of Lancaster (Henry IV). Henry V kept his nobles busy with wars in France, but under Henry VI they took sides again, fighting under the red rose of Lancaster or the white rose of York in the Wars of the Roses.

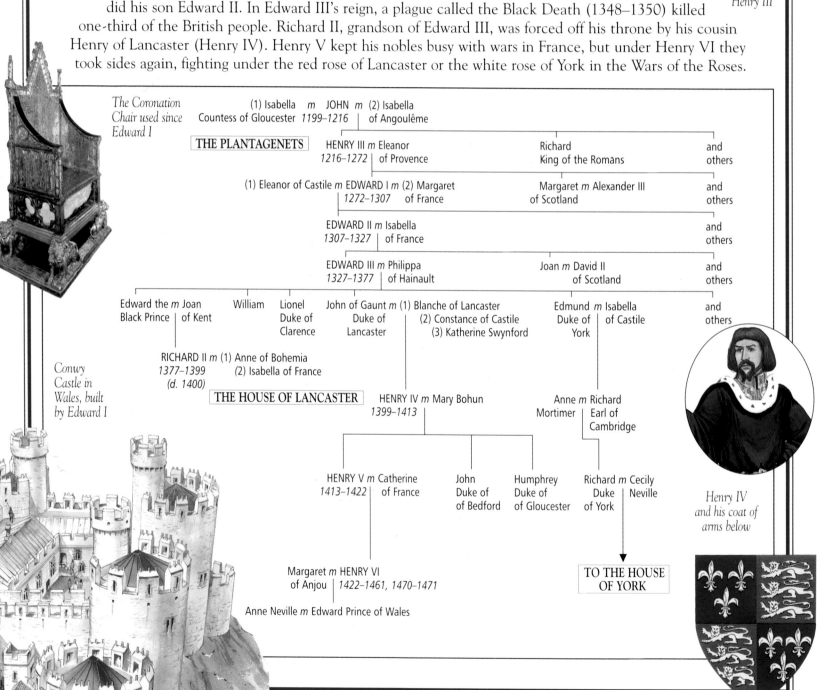

The Coronation Chair used since Edward I

Conwy Castle in Wales, built by Edward I

(1) Isabella   *m*   JOHN   *m*   (2) Isabella
Countess of Gloucester   *1199–1216*   of Angoulême

THE PLANTAGENETS

HENRY III *m* Eleanor   *1216–1272* of Provence

Richard King of the Romans   and others

(1) Eleanor of Castile *m* EDWARD I *m* (2) Margaret   *1272–1307* of France

Margaret *m* Alexander III of Scotland   and others

EDWARD II *m* Isabella   *1307–1327* of France   and others

EDWARD III *m* Philippa   *1327–1377* of Hainault

Joan *m* David II of Scotland   and others

Edward the *m* Joan
Black Prince | of Kent

William

Lionel Duke of Clarence

John of Gaunt *m* (1) Blanche of Lancaster
Duke of   (2) Constance of Castile
Lancaster   (3) Katherine Swynford

Edmund *m* Isabella
Duke of | of Castile
York

and others

RICHARD II *m* (1) Anne of Bohemia
1377–1399   (2) Isabella of France
(d. 1400)

THE HOUSE OF LANCASTER

HENRY IV *m* Mary Bohun
1399–1413

Anne *m* Richard
Mortimer | Earl of Cambridge

Henry IV and his coat of arms below

HENRY V *m* Catherine
1413–1422 | of France

John Duke of of Bedford

Humphrey Duke of Gloucester

Richard *m* Cecily
Duke | Neville
of York

→ TO THE HOUSE OF YORK

Margaret *m* HENRY VI
of Anjou | *1422–1461, 1470–1471*

Anne Neville *m* Edward Prince of Wales

THE HOUSE OF YORK AND THE TUDORS
1461–1603

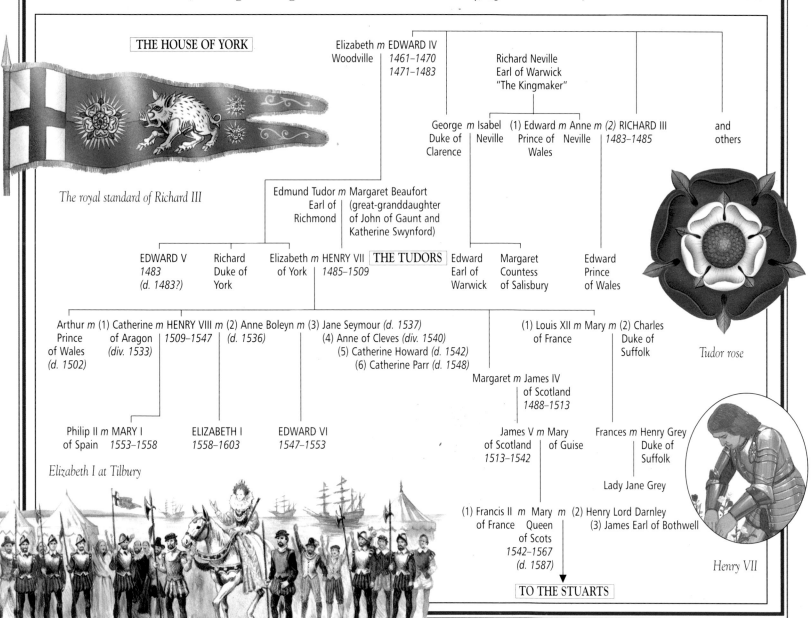

Edward IV

Edward IV was made king when the nobles on the side of York defeated those supporting Henry VI and Lancaster. Edward left a 12-year-old son, Edward V, but the boy was never crowned — he and his brother disappeared. Their uncle became Richard III. After only three years Henry Tudor claimed the throne. He defeated Richard at Bosworth, was crowned as Henry VII, and married Edward IV's daughter Elizabeth. The badges of the houses of York and Lancaster united in the Tudor rose. Henry VIII married six times but left only one son, Edward VI, who died young. Henry's daughter Mary I married Philip of Spain, the lifelong enemy of her sister, Elizabeth I. Elizabeth died childless, leaving the English crown to the son of Mary, Queen of Scots, the cousin she had executed.

The coat of arms of Edward IV and Henry VII

THE HOUSE OF YORK

Elizabeth *m* EDWARD IV
Woodville | *1461–1470*
1471–1483

Richard Neville
Earl of Warwick
"The Kingmaker"

George *m* Isabel | (1) Edward *m* Anne *m* (2) RICHARD III | and
Duke of | Neville | Prince of | Neville | *1483–1485* | others
Clarence | | Wales

The royal standard of Richard III

Edmund Tudor *m* Margaret Beaufort
Earl of | (great-granddaughter
Richmond | of John of Gaunt and
Katherine Swynford)

EDWARD V | Richard | Elizabeth *m* HENRY VII | THE TUDORS | Edward | Margaret | Edward
1483 | Duke of | of York | *1485–1509* | Earl of | Countess | Prince
(d. 1483?) | York | | | Warwick | of Salisbury | of Wales

Tudor rose

Arthur *m* (1) Catherine *m* HENRY VIII *m* (2) Anne Boleyn *m* (3) Jane Seymour *(d. 1537)*
Prince | of Aragon | *1509–1547* | *(d. 1536)* | (4) Anne of Cleves *(div. 1540)*
of Wales | *(div. 1533)* | | | (5) Catherine Howard *(d. 1542)*
(d. 1502) | | | | (6) Catherine Parr *(d. 1548)*

(1) Louis XII *m* Mary *m* (2) Charles
of France | | Duke of
| | Suffolk

Margaret *m* James IV
of Scotland
1488–1513

Philip II *m* MARY I | ELIZABETH I | EDWARD VI
of Spain | *1553–1558* | *1558–1603* | *1547–1553*

James V *m* Mary | Frances *m* Henry Grey
of Scotland | of Guise | Duke of
1513–1542 | | Suffolk

Lady Jane Grey

Elizabeth I at Tilbury

(1) Francis II *m* Mary *m* (2) Henry Lord Darnley
of France | Queen | (3) James Earl of Bothwell
| of Scots
| *1542–1567*
| *(d. 1587)*

TO THE STUARTS

Henry VII

CHARLES II
1660–1685
Bells and flowers joyfully welcomed home Charles as king after his exile in France during Cromwell's rule. Relaxed, witty and pleasure loving, he oversaw the recovery of London after the Plague (1665) and its rebuilding after the Great Fire (1666).

JAMES II
1685–1688
James's people distrusted his efforts to bring them to his own Roman Catholic faith. Finally they forced him to give up the crown.

GEORGE I
1714–1727
George, a Protestant German prince, was a distant cousin of Queen Anne. He let his ministers run the country. In his reign, Robert Walpole became first prime minister.

WILLIAM III
1688–1702 and
MARY II 1688–1694
When James II was sent into exile, his Protestant daughter Mary and her Dutch husband William were invited to become king and queen in his place. Mary died childless.

ANNE
1702–1714
Kind-hearted Anne, sister of Mary II, most enjoyed drinking tea with her friend Sarah Churchill. Sarah's soldier husband was made Duke of Marlborough after his victories against the French.

ALTH 60	CHARLES II 1660–1685		WILLIAM III 1688–1702	ANNE 1702–1714	GEORGE I 1714–1727	GEORGE II 1727–1760
		JAMES II 1685–1688	& MARY II 1688–1694			

THE HOUSE OF HANOVE

JAMES VI of Scotland 1567–1625 and I of England 1603–1625
James, son of Mary Queen of Scots, united the crowns of England and Scotland. Guy Fawkes' "Gunpowder Plot" luckily failed to kill him.

JAMES V
1513–1542
James was allied with France against the English. He died after Henry VIII's army defeated him in battle. His baby daughter Mary became Queen of Scotland.

MARY, QUEEN OF SCOTS
1542–1567
Educated in (and briefly Queen of) France, Mary was lovely but not wise. Driven out of Scotland at the age of 24, she fled to her cousin, Elizabeth I, who imprisoned her and after 20 years had her executed.

ELIZABETH I
1558–1603
Elizabeth was a great queen, celebrated by poets. Her sailors fought off Philip of Spain's invasion fleet, the Armada, and discovered new lands.

EDWARD VI
1547–1553
Henry VIII's six wives gave him only three children. Edward, the son of Henry's third wife, Jane Seymour, was never healthy and died when he was only 15 years old.

MARY I
1553–1558
The wife of Philip of Spain, Mary believed it her duty to make England Roman Catholic again. Many who disagreed had to die for their beliefs, including Archbishop Thomas Cranmer.

CHARLES I
1625–1649
Charles's struggle with Parliament over who should decide Britain's laws and religion led to the Civil War. Royalists fought Parliamentarians — and lost. The king was executed.

THE STUARTS
1603–1714

James I

In 1603 James VI of Scotland became the first Stuart king of England, James I. His son Charles I quarrelled so fiercely with Parliament that in 1642 Civil War broke out. Parliament's army, led by Oliver Cromwell, won and in 1649 the king was executed. His son Charles lived abroad during the period of Cromwell's rule — the Commonwealth — but returned as Charles II in 1660. His unpopular brother James II was driven out after only three years. James's daughter and her Dutch husband were invited to rule jointly as King William III and Queen Mary. (Later James's son, James Edward, would try in vain to get back the crown.) Queen Anne, James II's younger daughter, had 17 children, but they all died young, so she was the last Stuart ruler.

The coat of arms of James I

THE STUARTS

JAMES I *m* Anne
1603–1625 | of Denmark

Henry
Prince
of Wales

Elizabeth *m* Frederick V
Elector Palatine

CHARLES I *m* Henrietta Maria
1625–1649 | of France

and
others

Rupert
of the
Rhine

Sophia *m* Ernest Augustus
Elector of Hanover

CHARLES II *m* Catherine
1660–1685 of Braganza

Mary *m* William II
of Orange

(1) Anne Hyde *m* **JAMES II** *m* (2) Mary of Modena
1685–1688
(d. 1701)

and
others

WILLIAM III *m* **MARY II**
1688–1702 1688–1694

ANNE *m* George
1702–1714 of Denmark

TO THE HANOVERS

James Edward *m* Clementina
"The Old Pretender" | Sobieska

Louise

Charles Edward
"The Young Pretender"

Henry
Cardinal of York

---

*St. Edward's crown,
worn by Charles II*

English Civil War 1642–1651

THE HOUSE OF HANOVER
AND THE HOUSE OF
SAXE-COBURG GOTHA
1714–1910

George I

The coat of arms of George I

Geoorge, ruler of the small German state of Hanover, became King George I because most people did not want another Roman Catholic Stuart king. In 1715 James Edward, James II's Catholic son, failed to win back the throne. Under George II, in 1745, James Edward's son Charles ("Bonnie Prince Charlie") also failed, defeated at the Battle of Culloden. In George III's reign Britain's American colonies declared their independence (1776). For 10 years during George III's long illness, his eldest son ruled as Prince Regent before being crowned as George IV. After his brother William IV, their 18-year-old niece Victoria became Queen. She married Prince Albert of Saxe-Coburg Gotha and reigned for 63 years. Her eldest son, Edward VII, "The Peacemaker", helped to put off war in Europe.

Bonnie Prince Charlie's defeat at Culloden

The State Coach, built for George III

Edward VII and his coat of arms

THE HOUSE OF HANOVER

GEORGE I *m* Sophia Dorothea
1714–1727

GEORGE II *m* Caroline of
1727–1760 | Brandenburg-Ansbach

Frederick Louis *m* Augusta of
Prince of Wales | Saxe-Gotha

William
Duke of Cumberland

and others

GEORGE III *m* Charlotte
1760–1820 | of Mecklenburg-Strelitz

and others

GEORGE IV *m* Caroline
1820–1830 | of Brunswick

Frederick
Duke of York

WILLIAM IV *m* Adelaide of
1830–1837 | Saxe-Meiningen

Edward *m* Victoria of
Duke | Saxe-Coburg-
of Kent | Saalfield

Ernest Augustus
King of Hanover

and others

Charlotte

VICTORIA *m* Albert of
1837–1901 | Saxe-Coburg Gotha

THE HOUSE OF SAXE-COBURG GOTHA

Victoria *m* Frederick III
Princess | of Germany
Royal

EDWARD VII *m* Alexandra
1901–1910 | of Denmark

Alice

Alfred
Duke of
Edinburgh

Helena

Louise

Arthur
Duke of
Connaught

Leopold
Duke of
Albany

Beatrice *m* Henry of
Battenburg

Willhelm II
Emperor
of Germany

TO THE HOUSE OF WINDSOR

HOUSE OF SCOTLAND 1306–1625

JAMES I
1406–1437
James was seized by the English as a boy, and was 29 when he returned. He proved a fine, strong king — too strong for some of his lords, who murdered him.

JAMES II
1437–1460
Called "James of the Fiery Face" because of a birthmark, he loved the newly invented cannon. Eventually one killed him.

JAMES III
1460–1488
By James's marriage, the Orkney and Shetland Islands became part of Scotland. James was interested in astrology, poetry and music.

JAMES IV
1488–1513
Married to Margaret Tudor, sister of Henry VIII of England, James was clever, musical and attractive. He loved the Highlands and (unusually) could speak Gaelic.

HENRY V
1413–1422
Henry was a wild young prince, but a firm king, winning glory when his army defeated the French at Agincourt.

EDWARD IV
1461–1470
1471–1483
The final winner of the Wars of the Roses, Edward tried to restore order to the kingdom.

HENRY VIII
1509–1547
A brilliant young king, Henry later turned tyrannical. He married six times. While divorcing his first wife, he argued with the Pope and made himself Head of the new Church of England.

HENRY VI
1422–1461
1470–1471
Henry was a kindly man, but was often ill. During his reign, rival groups began battling for the crown, their badges the red rose of Lancaster and the white rose of York.

EDWARD V
1483 (never crowned)
Edward was probably only 12 years old when he and his younger brother, "the Princes in the Tower", were murdered.

RICHARD III
1483–1485
Was he really a "wicked uncle" who killed "the Princes in the Tower"? Nobody knows. He died in battle against Henry Tudor, who claimed his crown.

HENRY VII
1485–1509
Married to Edward IV's daughter Elizabeth, Henry Tudor kept England peaceful and made the country and the monarchy rich again.

ROBERT BRUCE 1306–1329	DAVID II 1329–1371	ROBERT II 1371–1390	ROBERT III 1390–1406	JAME 1406–

ROBERT BRUCE
1306–1329
Robert was a Scottish nobleman who fought to free Scotland from English rule. He beat the English army at Bannockburn and was at last crowned King of Scotland.

ROBERT II
1371–1390
Robert ruled the country while David II was away. He was old by the time he was crowned, and unable to control his nobles.

ROBERT III
1390–1406
Badly injured by a kick from a horse, Robert let his brother rule. The nobles continued to fight for power.

DAVID II 1329–1371
After losing a battle with the English, David was held in England for 11 years, where he enjoyed court life. The Scots paid a huge sum of gold for his return.

EDWARD III
1327–1377
Edward was a fighting king. His armies won many battles against the Scots and the French. He founded the Order of the Garter.

RICHARD II
1377–1399
Richard encouraged the first great English poet, Chaucer. Henry of Lancaster, a cousin of the king, seized the crown and had Richard murdered.

HENRY IV
1399–1413
Henry was haunted by the memory of Richard's murder. He faced rebellion in Wales and the north of England.

EDWARD II 1307–1327	EDWARD III 1327–1377	RICHARD II 1377–1399	HENRY IV 1399–1413	HENRY V 1413–1422

ETS 1216–1399

THE HOUSE OF WINDSOR
1910–

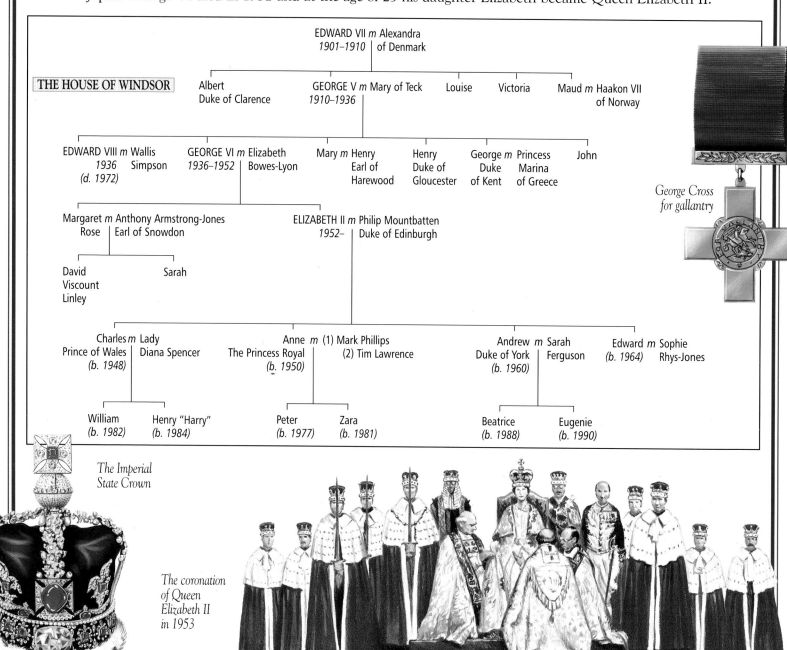

George V

In the reign of George V (son of Edward VII, "The Peacemaker"), the First World War broke out (1914–1918). Germany fought Britain, Russia, France and, from 1917, the United States; millions of soldiers were killed or wounded. When George V died, his eldest son, King Edward VIII, wanted to marry Mrs Wallis Simpson, a twice-divorced American whom some people felt should not be Queen. Refusing to rule without her, in 1936 Edward gave up the throne to his younger brother, George VI. In 1939 Adolf Hitler led Germany into the Second World War, which ended in 1945 when the first atomic bombs were dropped on Hitler's ally, Japan. George VI died in 1952 and at the age of 25 his daughter Elizabeth became Queen Elizabeth II.

The coat of arms of George V

EDWARD VII *m* Alexandra
1901–1910 | of Denmark

THE HOUSE OF WINDSOR

Albert
Duke of Clarence

GEORGE V *m* Mary of Teck
1910–1936

Louise

Victoria

Maud *m* Haakon VII
of Norway

EDWARD VIII *m* Wallis
1936 Simpson
(d. 1972)

GEORGE VI *m* Elizabeth
1936–1952 | Bowes-Lyon

Mary *m* Henry
Earl of
Harewood

Henry
Duke of
Gloucester

George *m* Princess
Duke Marina
of Kent of Greece

John

Margaret *m* Anthony Armstrong-Jones
Rose | Earl of Snowdon

ELIZABETH II *m* Philip Mountbatten
1952– | Duke of Edinburgh

David
Viscount
Linley

Sarah

*George Cross
for gallantry*

Charles *m* Lady
Prince of Wales | Diana Spencer
(b. 1948)

Anne *m* (1) Mark Phillips
The Princess Royal (2) Tim Lawrence
(b. 1950)

Andrew *m* Sarah
Duke of York | Ferguson
(b. 1960)

Edward *m* Sophie
(b. 1964) Rhys-Jones

William
(b. 1982)

Henry "Harry"
(b. 1984)

Peter
(b. 1977)

Zara
(b. 1981)

Beatrice
(b. 1988)

Eugenie
(b. 1990)

*The Imperial
State Crown*

*The coronation
of Queen
Elizabeth II
in 1953*

RICHARD I 1189–1199
Visiting England for only four months, this great soldier, "The Lionheart", spent his 10-year reign in Palestine, fighting Saladin's Muslim army in the Crusades.

JOHN 1199–1216
King John was forced by his nobles in 1215 to set his seal on, or "sign", the Magna Carta, the "Great Charter", which still binds English rulers "to refuse justice to none".

HENRY III 1216–1272
Henry took as his family badge a sprig of broom, called *Planta genista* in Latin, giving the family its name: the Plantagenets. He loved art and architecture, and built the Westminster Abbey we see today in London.

EDWARD II 1307–1327
Edward's foolishness and extravagance at court drove his French wife to raise an army to try and take over the kingdom. He was murdered by his jailers in Berkeley Castle, in Gloucestershire.

EDWARD I 1272–1307
Edward was called "The Hammer of the Scots" for his wars with Scotland's king, Robert Bruce. He made his son, born at Caernarvon, the first English Prince of Wales.

RICHARD I 1189–1199	JOHN 1199–1216	HENRY III 1216–1272	EDWARD I 1272–1307
1154–1216			THE PLANTAG

THE ROYAL HOUSE OF SCOTLAND
1306–1625

Robert I

The wax seal of Robert I

By 1306 the Scottish royal line had died out, leaving the throne empty and claimed by a dozen lords. One of them, Robert Bruce, was chosen to be king and the title stayed with his family. He was succeeded by his son, David II. The next ruler, Robert II, was the child of Bruce's daughter Margery and Walter Fitz Alan, the High Steward (or Stewart) of Scotland. He was the first of the Stewart rulers. Five others followed before James V succeeded. When in 1542 James V said on his deathbed of the crown of Scotland, "It came with a lass, it will go with a lass", he was thinking of long-ago Margery and of his own week-old daughter Mary, Queen of Scots. Mary's son James VI was indeed the last independent King of Scotland.

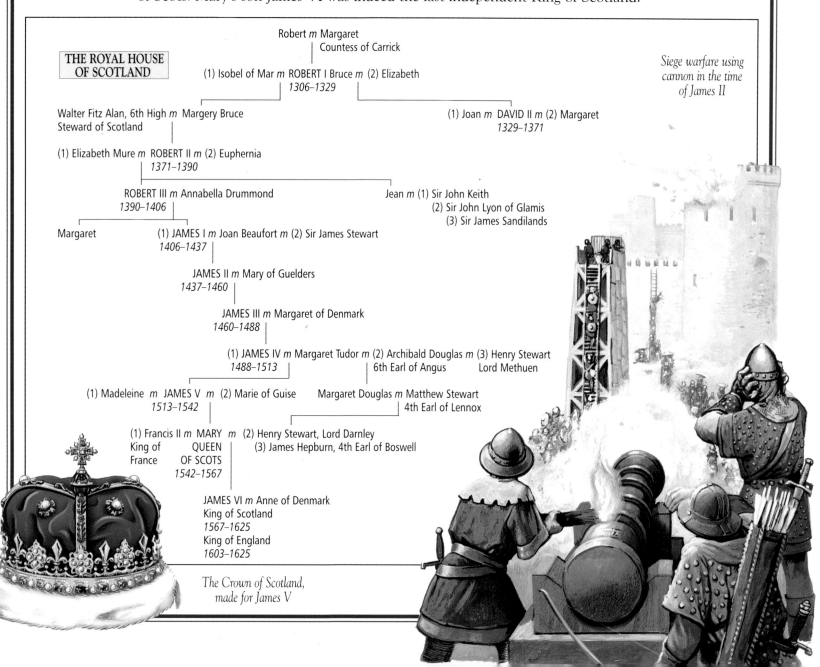

THE ROYAL HOUSE OF SCOTLAND

Siege warfare using cannon in the time of James II

Robert *m* Margaret
Countess of Carrick

(1) Isobel of Mar *m* ROBERT I Bruce *m* (2) Elizabeth
1306–1329

(1) Joan *m* DAVID II *m* (2) Margaret
1329–1371

Walter Fitz Alan, 6th High *m* Margery Bruce
Steward of Scotland

(1) Elizabeth Mure *m* ROBERT II *m* (2) Euphernia
1371–1390

ROBERT III *m* Annabella Drummond
1390–1406

Jean *m* (1) Sir John Keith
(2) Sir John Lyon of Glamis
(3) Sir James Sandilands

Margaret

(1) JAMES I *m* Joan Beaufort *m* (2) Sir James Stewart
1406–1437

JAMES II *m* Mary of Guelders
1437–1460

JAMES III *m* Margaret of Denmark
1460–1488

(1) JAMES IV *m* Margaret Tudor *m* (2) Archibald Douglas *m* (3) Henry Stewart
1488–1513 6th Earl of Angus Lord Methuen

(1) Madeleine *m* JAMES V *m* (2) Marie of Guise
1513–1542

Margaret Douglas *m* Matthew Stewart
4th Earl of Lennox

(1) Francis II *m* MARY *m* (2) Henry Stewart, Lord Darnley
King of QUEEN (3) James Hepburn, 4th Earl of Boswell
France OF SCOTS
1542–1567

JAMES VI *m* Anne of Denmark
King of Scotland
1567–1625
King of England
1603–1625

The Crown of Scotland, made for James V